cooking the Polish way

Although the ingredients in hunter's stew vary from family to family, this traditional dish is always a Polish favorite. (Recipe on page 18.)

cooking the Polish way

DANUTA ZAMOJSKA-HUTCHINS

PHOTOGRAPHS BY ROBERT L. & DIANE WOLFE

easy menu *ethnic* cookbooks

Lerner Publications Company ■ Minneapolis

Editor: Emily Blackburn Kelley

Drawings and Map by Jeanette Swofford

The page border for this book is based on the poppy, one of Poland's most popular flowers.

To Edward and Maria and all the children eager to learn about other cultures. Such knowledge is a way to world peace and friendship.

Library of Congress Cataloging in Publication Data

Zamojska-Hutchins, Danuta.
   Cooking the Polish way.

   (Easy menu ethnic cookbooks)
   Includes index.
   Summary: An introduction to the cooking of Poland, featuring traditional recipes for lunch, appetizers, dinner, and desserts. Also includes information on the geography, customs, and people of Poland.
   1. Cookery, Polish—Juvenile literature. [1. Cookery, Polish] I. Wolfe, Robert L., ill. II. Wolfe, Diane, ill. III. Swofford, Jeanette, ill. IV. Title. V. Series.
TX723.5.P6Z3   1984   641.59438   84-11226
ISBN 0-8225-0909-1 (lib. bdg.)

Manufactured in the United States of America

      3   4   5   6   7   8   9   10   93   92   91

Royal *mazurek* is a good example of the care that is taken by Polish people in decorating food. (Recipe on page 45.)

CONTENTS

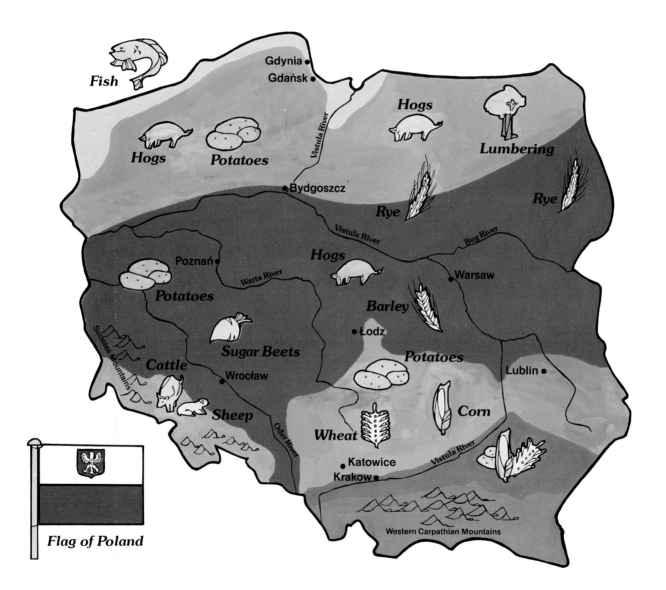

Fish

Gdynia
Gdańsk

Hogs

Hogs
Potatoes

Vistula River

Lumbering

Bydgoszcz

Rye

Vistula River

Rye

Bug River

Hogs

Poznań

Warsaw

Warta River

Potatoes

Barley

Sudetes Mountains

Lodz

Cattle

Sugar Beets

Potatoes

Lublin

Wrocław

Sheep

Odra River

Corn

Wheat

Katowice

Vistula River

Krakow

Western Carpathian Mountains

Flag of Poland

INTRODUCTION

Polish people, whether living in Poland or in other parts of the world, have a fierce love for their country. They pride themselves on a strong national identity, something they have had to struggle to keep throughout many different times in their nation's thousand-year history. Food, which has often been scarce in Poland, is a very important part of the Polish heritage. Preparing and eating food in Poland marks most social occasions, particularly family get-togethers. Such gatherings often celebrate name days or the church holidays that are a part of Poland's long-standing Roman Catholic tradition. Polish cooking is rich, hearty, and varied in its many flavors and textures. Over hundreds of years, it has been influenced by many things, including a strong farming tradition, Poland's natural resources, and many contacts with other cultures.

THE LAND

The name Poland comes from the Polish word for "fields" or "plains" (*pola*), since much of the country is flat. Located in central Europe, Poland is bordered by the Baltic Sea to the north, the Soviet Union to the east, Czechoslovakia to the south, and Germany to the west.

The Baltic coast of Poland is made up of sandy beaches, sand dunes, and high, forested shores. Poland's major seaport, Gdansk, is located on this coast. Directly south of the Baltic coast is the Pomeranian and Mazurian lakes region. It is a popular vacation spot because of the many beautiful lakes and forests found there. The central plains in the middle of the country make up Poland's largest agricultural area. The present-day capital of Poland, Warsaw, is located here on the banks of the Vistula River. Halfway between Warsaw and Poland's southern border, the land gradually rises. First come the low, ancient mountains and broad valleys. In western and south-central Poland are higher hills and the most densely populated areas of the country. In southeastern Poland are rolling hills covered with fruit orchards and forests. The southernmost part of Poland rises steeply into the rugged, wild Tatra Mountains—part of the

Carpathian mountain range—where several national parks can be found. The people who live in this region are different from any other in Poland. They have managed to preserve their regional dialect, dress, and traditional occupation of raising sheep. They are known for their sheep-milk products and hand-spun wool as well as for their primitive wood sculptures, tapestries, and glass paintings, which are often exported to the United States.

THE FOOD

The Baltic Sea, along with many inland lakes and rivers, means an abundance of seafood, including flounder, salmon, trout, and the North Sea herring, all of which are caught by Polish fishermen. Wheat, rye, barley, potatoes, sugar beets, and sunflowers are grown on much of the rich farmland in Poland, so it is no surprise that Poles eat a lot of bread, noodles, potatoes, and barley groats. Many people also grow their own beets, cabbage, and carrots, three important foods in Polish cooking. Meat is not eaten in great quantity in Poland, but the most common meat found on Polish tables is pork because of the abundance at one time of wild boars.

Poland was once ruled by kings and queens, many of whom married foreign princesses and princes. With each foreign marriage came a new cuisine. Hungarian goulash, Italian vegetables and macaroni, French pastries, and Ukrainian beet soup have all found their way into Polish cooking. Over the years, however, the Polish people have adapted these foreign foods to suit their own tastes, and a unique Polish cuisine has been the result.

CUSTOMS

Over ninety percent of Poland's people are Roman Catholics who have long observed religious fasts. Because no meat is eaten during these fasts, they have developed a great variety of delicious fish and meatless dishes. Fasting and feasting go hand in hand in Poland, for at the end of each *fast* is a tremendous *feast!* Christmas Eve day is a day of fasting. The only meal eaten is dinner, which begins when the evening star appears.

This was always a wonderful holiday when

I was growing up. During the afternoon, we children helped trim the Christmas tree with decorations we had made ourselves. Just before dinner, Santa Claus secretly hid presents for us while we were busy helping with the evening meal.

Our Christmas Eve table was covered with a beautiful, snow-white linen cloth. Underneath the cloth was a small bundle of hay, symbolizing our good deeds during Advent. In the center of the table was the *Opłatek Wigilijny* (op-WAH-tehk vee-gee-LEEY-nih), the Christmas wafer that we shared while offering good wishes to one another. An extra place was always set at the table on this night for any unexpected visitor.

At last it was time for the carefully prepared dinner, which consisted of as many as 21 traditional courses. Every bite of the meal was savored and enjoyed by all.

After the meal was over, we sang Christmas carols and opened gifts. Everyone waited with great anticipation for the Pasterka (pahs-TER-kah), the Shepherd's Mass, which began at midnight and didn't end until after 2:00 A.M. on Christmas morning.

THE PEOPLE

If there is one word that describes the Polish people it's hospitality. A Polish proverb, *Gość w dom, Bòg w dom* ("A guest in the home is God in the home."), is taken very seriously by most Poles. To be a guest in a Polish home is to be treated like royalty, and food is always served. An unannounced guest can expect at least tea and pastries. (Unexpected visitors are fairly common in Poland where many people do not have telephones.) Guests who have been invited to a Polish home for dinner will probably sit down to a seven- or eight-course meal!

Although you may not be making many seven-course meals, you should make each recipe in this book with great care. Then, when you serve the food, do as the Poles do and sit down with your family or friends and enjoy every bite of food as well as some friendly conversation. As the Poles say, "smacznego" (smatch-NAY-goh), which means "have a tasty meal!"

A Polish table is always an inviting place to sit and enjoy good food and conversation.

A POLISH TABLE

A Polish table reflects the importance of mealtime in Poland. It is always pleasant to look at and an enjoyable place to sit down. Linen tablecloths or handmade placemats are used along with cloth napkins and simple place settings of silverware. Freshly cut flowers are on the table the year round, and, for special occasions, a small vase of flowers is put at each place.

For most meals, food is placed in china serving dishes that are passed from person to person and then placed in the center of the table. For larger, more formal dinners, the food is often served buffet style.

Several condiments are found on Polish tables, including salt, pepper, and horseradish. Fresh-fruit compote is often included on the dinner table to accompany the main dish.

All of these things combine to make a warm, comfortable atmosphere in which diners can relax and enjoy each tasty meal.

BEFORE YOU BEGIN

Cooking any dish, plain or fancy, is easier and more fun if you are familiar with its ingredients. Polish cooking makes use of some ingredients that you may not know. You should also be familiar with the special terms that will be used in various recipes in this book. Therefore, *before* you start cooking any of the Polish dishes in this book, study the following "dictionary" of special ingredients and terms very carefully. Then read through the recipe you want to try from beginning to end.

Now you are ready to shop for ingredients and to organize the cookware you will need. Once you have assembled everything, you can begin to cook. It is also important to read *The Careful Cook* on page 48 before you start.

COOKING UTENSILS

colander — A bowl with holes in the bottom and sides. It is used for draining liquid from a solid food.

double boiler — A utensil made up of two pans that fit together. Heat from the water boiling in the lower pan cooks food in the upper pan without scorching.

Dutch oven — A heavy pot with a tight-fitting domed lid that is often used for cooking soups or stews

slotted spoon — A spoon with small openings in the bowl. It is used to pick solid food out of a liquid.

COOKING TERMS

baste — To pour or spoon liquid over food as it roasts in order to flavor and moisten it

boil — To heat a liquid over high heat until bubbles form and rise rapidly to the surface

core — To remove the center part of a fruit or vegetable that contains the stem and/or seeds

cream — To beat several ingredients together until the mixture has a smooth consistency

florets — Individual, flower-like pieces that group together to form the heads of such vegetables as cauliflower and broccoli

grate — To cut into tiny pieces by rubbing the food against a grater

knead — To work dough by pressing it with the palms, pushing it outward, and then pressing it over on itself

pinch — A very small amount, usually what you can pick up between your thumb and forefinger

preheat — To allow an oven to warm up to a certain temperature before putting food in it

shred — To cut into tiny pieces with a knife

simmer — To cook over low heat in liquid kept just below its boiling point. Bubbles may occasionally rise to the surface.

whip — To beat cream, gelatin, or egg white at high speed until light and fluffy in texture

SPECIAL INGREDIENTS

allspice — The berry of a West Indian tree. It is used whole or ground in cooking to give a slightly sweet flavor to food.

almond extract — A liquid made from almonds that is used in baking

bread crumbs — Tiny pieces of stale bread made by crushing the bread with the bottom of a glass or a rolling pin. Packaged bread crumbs can be bought at grocery stores.

candied orange peel — Orange peel that has been cooked in sugar or syrup until it has crystallized

citron — A thick-skinned, yellow fruit that is similar to a lemon or lime. The candied rind of this fruit is used in baking.

Dijon-style mustard — A commercially prepared condiment (ingredient used to enhance the flavor of food) made from mustard seed, white wine, vinegar, salt, and spices

dried mushrooms — Fresh mushrooms that have been dried. They have a leathery texture and are usually used in soups or other foods in which they can soak up liquid.

kohlrabi — A light-green vegetable in the cabbage family

marjoram — An herb related to mint that is used in cooking. It is known for its sweet aroma and flavor.

parsnip — The long, white, sweet-tasting root vegetable of the parsnip plant

pearl barley — Seeds of the barley plant that have been rubbed into smooth, round grains. It is usually used in soups and ground-meat dishes.

peppercorns — The berries of an East Indian plant. Peppercorns are used both whole and ground (pepper) to flavor food.

poppy seed pastry filling — A thick, sweet mixture made from poppy seeds and corn syrup that is used in making pies, cakes, and breads

rutabaga — The edible, yellow root vegetable of a plant similar to the turnip

white-wine vinegar — Vinegar made from white wine. It has a sharp, tangy flavor.

A POLISH MENU

Below is a menu for a typical day of Polish cooking. The Polish names of the dishes are given, along with a guide on how to pronounce them. *Recipe included in book*

ENGLISH	PO POLSKU	PRONUNCIATION
MENU	MENÚ	meh-NEW
Breakfast	**Śniadanie**	shnya-DAH-nyeh
Oatmeal	Płatki owsiane	PWAT-kee off-SYAH-neh
Bagel with cream cheese	Bajgieł z twarożkiem	BY-gew stfa-ROZH-kyem
Sliced meats	Wędlina	vend-LIH-nah
Bread with butter	Chleb z masłcm	HLEP ZMΛS-wem
Farmer's cheese	Ser biały	SER BYAH-wih
Second Breakfast	**Drugie sniadanie**	DROO-gyeh shnya-DAH-nyeh
I	I	
*Hunter's stew	Bigos	BEE-gos
Bread with Swiss cheese	Chleb z serem szwajcarskim	HLEP s-SEH-rem shfay-TSAR-skim
Pear	Gruszka	GROOH-shkee
Tea	Herbata	her-BAH-tah
II	II	
*Herring paste on bread	Kanapki z pasty śledziowej	kah-NAP-kee SPAS-tih shleh-DJO-vay
Cucumber (raw)	Ogórek	oh-GHOOR-ek
*Mushrooms in vinegar	Grzybki w occie	GZHIP-kee VOTS-tsyeh
*Barley soup	Krupnik polski	KROOP-nik POL-skih
Milk	Mleko	MLEH-koh
Dinner	**Obiad**	OH-byat
I	I	
*Eggplant caviar	Kawior z bakłażana	KAH-vyor zbah-kwah-ZHAH-nah
*Pierożki	Pierożki	pyeh-ROZH-kee

ENGLISH	PO POLSKU	PRONUNCIATION
Plum and rhubarb soup	Zupa śliwkowo rabarbarowa	ZOO-pah shleef-KOH-voh rah-bar-bah-ROH-vah
Bread	Chleb	HLEP
*Chicken Polish style	Kurczę po polsku	KOOR-chen poh-POL-skoo
*Rutabagas and carrots	Brukiew z marchwią zasmażana	BROO-kyief ZMAR-hfyom zah-smah-ZHAH-nah
*Vegetable salad	Sałatka z jarzyn	sah-WAT-kah ZYA-zhin
*Noodles with poppy seed	Kluski z makiem	KLOO-skih ZMAH-kyem
Tea	Herbata	her-BAH-tah
II	II	
*Eggs stuffed with ham	Jajka nadziewane szynką	YAY-kah nah-dje-VAH-neh SHIN-kom
*Spring vegetable soup	Zupa wiosenna	ZOO-pah vyoh-SEN-nah
Bread	Chleb	HLEP
*Roast stuffed fish	Ryba nadziewana pieczona	RIH-bah nah-djeh-WAH-nah pyeh-CHONA-nah
*Cauliflower with Polish sauce	Kalafior w sosie polskim	kah-LAH-fyor FSOH-shyeh POL-skeem
*Tomato and Onion Tier Salad	Sałatka z pomidorów z cebulą	sah-WAT-kah spo-mee-DOH-roof stseh-BOO-lom
*Semi-short bread with plums or apricots	Placek pótkruchy ze śliwkami lub z morelami	PLAH-tsek poow-KROO-hih zeh-sheef-KAH-mee loop zmoh-reh-LAH-mee
Tea with lemon	Herbata z cytryną	her-BAH-tah stsit-RIH-nom
Supper	*Kolacja*	koh-LAH-tsyah
I	I	
Bread with Edam cheese	Chleb z serem edamskim	HLEP s-SEH-rem eh-DAM-skim
*Cucumbers in sour cream	Mizeria	Mee-ZEH-rya
*"Little pigeons" in tomato sauce	Gołabki	goh-WOMP-kee
*Royal mazurek	Mazurek królewski	mah-ZOO-rehk krooh-LEF-skee
Oat cocoa	Kakao owsiane	kah-KAH-oh off-SYAH-neh
II	II	
Bread	Chleb	HLEP
Sliced meats	Wędlina	vend-LIH-nah
*Vegetable garni	Bukiet z jarzyn	BOO-kyet ZYAH-zhin
*Carrot gingerbread	Piernik z marchwi	PYER-nik ZMAR-hfee
Oat cocoa	Kakao owsiane	kah-KAH-oh off-SYAH-neh

BREAKFAST

Breakfast in Poland is a hearty, filling meal, especially in the winter when it's snowy and cold. It gives people the energy they need to start the day. Breakfast is usually eaten between 6:00 and 8:00 A.M. In the winter, oatmeal, hot wheat cereal, or *grysik* (GRIH-shik) (millet) is usually served along with bread and butter, bagels and cream cheese, sliced meats, and mild cheeses. Summertime breakfasts are usually a bit lighter, consisting of cream cheese and bagels, croissants and jam, bread and butter, and sliced meats and cheeses. Accompanying breakfast at any time of the year are grain coffee with chicory for adults and warm milk or oat cocoa for children. Grain coffee is made from roasted wheat or barley and is often mixed with the ground, roasted root of the chicory plant. Oat cocoa is a hot drink made from roasted oatmeal.

SECOND BREAKFAST

Between 11:00 A.M. and 1:00 P.M., second breakfast is eaten by people who have only a short break from work and by school children. Those who have a longer break at midday often go home or eat in a milk bar, which is a restaurant offering only meatless, milk-based dishes. Second breakfast usually consists of an open-face sandwich, hot homemade soup, a raw vegetable such as a cucumber, and fruit.

Barley Soup

1 medium potato
1 carrot
4 10¾-ounce cans (about 6
　cups) beef broth
½ tablespoon dried parsley flakes
½ tablespoon dill weed
2 or 3 fresh mushrooms (optional)
¼ cup pearl barley
1 teaspoon butter or margarine
¼ cup whipping cream or half and half
　(optional)

1. Peel potato and carrot and cut into bite-size pieces.

2. Put all but ¾ cup broth into a large kettle. Add potato, carrot, parsley flakes, and dill weed and bring to a boil. Reduce heat to low and cover.

3. Meanwhile, clean and slice mushrooms. Melt butter in skillet over medium heat. Add barley and mushrooms and sauté 1 to 2 minutes. Add remaining broth and simmer 5 to 7 minutes or until mushrooms are soft.

4. Add barley mixture to kettle and simmer for about 45 minutes or until barley is tender.

5. Serve hot soup plain, or stir ¼ cup cream into it just before serving.

Serves 4 to 6

Barley, vegetables, and beef broth make a delicious soup that can be eaten for second breakfast, dinner, or supper.

Hunter's Stew

Hunter's stew has been the Polish national dish for hundreds of years. This tempting stew can be eaten hot or cold. It is delicious when reheated, and the leftovers can be frozen for future use.

In Poland, venison is commonly used in hunter's stew, but if it is not available, you can substitute ½ pound of beef or an additional ¼ pound each of beef and pork. All the meat will be much easier to cut if it is slightly frozen.

1 16-ounce jar sauerkraut
½ cup (1 stick) butter or margarine or ½ cup bacon fat
2 dried mushrooms, crushed (optional)
½ teaspoon salt
1 teaspoon black pepper
1 teaspoon marjoram
1 teaspoon dried parsley flakes
1 teaspoon basil
⅛ teaspoon cayenne pepper (optional)
2 tablespoons paprika
2 or 3 cloves garlic, minced
1 6-ounce can tomato paste
1 tablespoon sugar
6 to 8 pitted, dried prunes
1 small head cabbage
5 cups water
2 large green apples
2 carrots
2 medium tomatoes
1 medium onion
½ pound each boneless stewing beef, pork, and venison
½ pound each smoked ham and smoked Polish sausage
½ cup all-purpose flour

1. Preheat oven to 325°.
2. Place sauerkraut in colander to drain. Using your hands, squeeze out any remaining liquid. Chop sauerkraut into smaller pieces.
3. Melt ¼ cup fat in a large skillet. Add sauerkraut, mushrooms, spices, garlic, tomato paste, and sugar and fry for 10 minutes over medium heat. Remove from heat and set aside.
4. Chop prunes into small pieces. Core, wash, and shred cabbage. Peel, core, and chop apples into bite-size pieces. Peel and

grate carrots. Peel and chop tomatoes and onion into small pieces.

5. Place water and all ingredients from step 4 in a Dutch oven. Cover and put on middle oven rack to begin cooking.

6. Cut all meat into bite-size pieces. Put flour into a clean paper bag. Place cubes of meat (except ham and Polish sausage) into bag, about ¼ pound at a time, and shake to coat meat.

7. Melt remaining ¼ cup fat in a large skillet or heavy pot and brown meat (except ham and sausage) on all sides over medium-high heat.

8. Add meat, ham and sausage, and sauerkraut mixture from step 3 to Dutch oven and mix well.

9. Return stew to oven and cook for 2 to 2½ hours or until meat is tender.

10. Serve stew steaming hot in individual bowls along with bread, mashed potatoes, or rice.

Serves 8 to 10

Herring Paste

2 hard-cooked eggs
1 8-ounce jar marinated herring fillets, drained (any kind)
¼ cup butter or margarine, softened

1. Hard cook eggs by placing in a saucepan and covering with cold water. Place over medium heat until boiling, reduce heat, and simmer for 15 minutes. Drain water from saucepan and run cold water over eggs until they are cool.

2. Peel cooked eggs. Cut in half lengthwise and remove yolks.

3. Put herring, hard-cooked egg yolks, and butter in blender and blend until smooth. (If you don't have a blender, cut herring into very small pieces and place in bowl. Add egg yolks and butter and mash with a fork.)

4. Spoon herring into serving dish. Decorate with pieces of hard-cooked egg white and serve with thinly sliced rye or pumpernickel bread.

Makes 1½ cups

Mushrooms in Vinegar

This popular appetizer is made with very fresh mushrooms in Poland, where people often pick their own in the country's many forests. It will keep for up to two months in the refrigerator.

2 cups white-wine vinegar
3 tablespoons sugar
1 teaspoon salt
¼ teaspoon peppercorns
¼ teaspoon whole allspice
1 clove garlic
2 bay leaves
2 pounds fresh mushrooms
1 small onion

1. Put vinegar, sugar, spices, garlic, and bay leaves in a saucepan. Bring to a boil, then remove from heat and cool.
2. Clean mushrooms and trim off ends. (Do not remove whole stem.) Peel onion.
3. Put 6 cups water and 1 teaspoon salt in saucepan and bring to a boil. Add mushrooms and whole onion and boil 3 to 4 minutes. Remove from heat, drain, and let cool.
4. Put 3 tablespoons vinegar mixture into each of 2 quart jars. Divide mushrooms equally and put into jars. Slice boiled onion and place on top of mushrooms. Fill each jar with remaining vinegar mixture.
5. Cover jars tightly and place in refrigerator until ready to serve.

Makes 2 quarts

DINNER

Dinner is the main meal of the day in Poland and is eaten between 4:30 and 6:00 P.M. when all of the family members are home from work and school. The Polish people have very strong family ties, so dinner is an especially important time for them. It is the one time of the day when each family member can share the day's events with the others. At a Polish dinner table, one can find friendly conversation, family togetherness, and mouth-watering food.

Eggplant Caviar

This tasty appetizer takes its name from something quite different than eggplant. Real caviar is made from the eggs of sturgeon, salmon, and other kinds of fish! It is a highly prized food in many parts of the world and is very expensive. You will enjoy this less expensive imitation.

If you use fresh parsley, cut it with a clean pair of scissors.

1 small eggplant
1 small onion
2 medium tomatoes
2 tablespoons olive or vegetable oil
2 tablespoons lemon juice
½ teaspoon salt
¼ teaspoon pepper
2 sprigs fresh parsley or 1 teaspoon dried parsley flakes

1. Preheat oven to 375°.
2. Pierce eggplant a few times with a fork. Place eggplant on a cookie sheet and bake whole for about 45 minutes or until tender. (Eggplant is done when a fork can easily be inserted into it.)
3. When eggplant is cool, peel and chop.
4. Peel and chop onion. Wash and chop tomatoes and parsley.
5. In a mixing bowl, combine eggplant, onion, tomato, oil, lemon juice, salt, and pepper. Mix well and chill.
6. Put eggplant mixture in a serving dish and sprinkle with parsley. Serve with small pieces of bread or crackers.

Makes 2 to 3 cups

Herring paste and eggs stuffed with ham can be eaten either as appetizers before dinner or as part of second breakfast.

Eggs Stuffed with Ham

The leftovers of this delicious filling can be used as sandwich spread or for making pieroŻkis.

4 hard-cooked eggs
½ pound cooked ham
¼ cup grated Monterey Jack cheese
4 tablespoons sour cream
2 teaspoons Dijon-style mustard
⅛ teaspoon pepper

1. See page 19 for directions for cooking eggs.
2. Peel eggs. Cut in half lengthwise and remove yolks. Cut off a small slice of the rounded part of each egg half so they will sit flat on a plate.
3. Chop ham into very small pieces.
4. Blend ham, cheese, egg yolks, sour cream, mustard, and pepper with a fork.
5. Stuff each egg half with ham mixture. Arrange on a serving plate and top each one with a small dab of mayonnaise.

Makes 8 stuffed eggs

Pierożki (also called *pierogi*) is often eaten with a salad and bread for a delicious light meal. (Recipe on page 24.)

Pierożki

Sauerkraut Filling:

4 ounces sauerkraut, drained
2 tablespoons bacon fat, butter, or
　　margarine
½ onion, peeled and chopped
¼ teaspoon paprika
¼ teaspoon salt
¼ teaspoon pepper
¼ teaspoon marjoram

1. Chop sauerkraut into very small pieces.
2. Melt fat in skillet. Add sauerkraut and remaining ingredients and fry over low heat for about 10 minutes, stirring occasionally.
3. Fill and cook *pierożkis* as directed.

Savory Cheese Filling:

8 ounces (1 cup) cottage cheese
2 tablespoons bread crumbs
1 egg yolk
½ teaspoon salt
¼ teaspoon pepper
　　pinch of garlic powder (optional)

1. Put all ingredients in medium bowl and mix well.
2. Fill and cook *pierożkis* as directed.

Dough:

2 cups all-purpose flour
1 egg
⅛ teaspoon salt
½ to ¾ cup water or skim milk

1. In a medium bowl, mix together flour, salt, and egg. Add liquid, a little at a time, until dough is stiff.
2. Knead dough for 2 to 4 minutes on a floured surface. (You will have to add more flour.) Roll out dough to ⅛-inch thickness with a rolling pin.
3. With a glass or cookie cutter, cut out rounds of dough 3 inches in diameter.
4. Put 1 tablespoon filling on one half of each circle.
5. Moisten edges of dough with a little water. Fold dough over filling and press edges together first with your fingers, then with the tines of a fork.

6. Fill a large kettle with water and 1 teaspoon salt and bring to a boil. Place *pierożkis* in boiling water a few at a time. (If you put too many in the kettle at once, they will stick together.) Boil for 3 to 5 minutes or until *pierożkis* begin to float.

7. Sprinkle *pierożkis* with grated Parmesan or Romano cheese and serve.

Makes 12 to 18 pierożkis

Spring Vegetable Soup

½ **medium head cauliflower**
2 **medium potatoes**
2 **carrots**
2 **kohlrabi (optional)**
3 **or 4 green onions**
4 **10¾-ounce cans (about 6 cups) chicken broth**
1 **teaspoon dried parsley flakes**
1 **teaspoon dill weed**
1 **tablespoon butter or margarine**

1. Remove cauliflower florets from stem and wash. Wash and peel potatoes, carrots, and kohlrabi. Trim green onions. Cut all vegetables into bite-size pieces.

2. Put broth and vegetables into large kettle and bring to a boil. Reduce heat and simmer uncovered about 20 minutes or until vegetables are tender but not mushy.

3. Just before serving, add parsley flakes, dill weed, and butter.

4. Serve hot soup in bowls along with bread.

Serves 6 to 8

Polish people eat a wide variety of soups including hearty spring vegetable soup *(left)* and rich fruit soup made with plums and rhubarb.

Plum and Rhubarb Soup

This delicious fruit soup is easy to make and can be eaten either hot at the beginning of a meal or cold for dessert.

Dried, pitted prunes can be used instead of plums, and tart green apples can be substituted for rhubarb. If you use apples, peel and core them. If you use prunes, cover them with water and soak overnight. The liquid can then be used in the soup.

½ pound plums or pitted, dried prunes
½ pound rhubarb or tart green apples
6 cups water
3 or 4 whole cloves
1 small stick cinnamon
¼ cup sugar
2 tablespoons all-purpose flour
   or cornstarch
½ cup sour cream

1. Wash fruit. Remove pits and stems from plums. Remove ends and tops of rhubarb. Chop fruit into chunks.
2. Combine fruit, water, cloves, cinnamon, and sugar in a large kettle. Bring to a boil, then cover, reduce heat, and simmer for 10 to 15 minutes.
3. Remove cloves and cinnamon with a slotted spoon and discard.
4. Remove half of fruit with slotted spoon and mash with a fork.
5. In a cup, add ¼ cup cold water to flour or cornstarch, a little at a time, to make a thick paste.
6. Add paste to the mashed fruit, then return fruit to kettle and bring to a boil.
7. As soon as soup begins to boil, remove from heat and let stand for 3 or 4 minutes.
8. Serve soup hot or cold with dollops of sour cream on top.

Serves 6 to 8

Tomato and onion tier salad *(left)* **and vegetable salad are especially good in hot weather.**

Vegetable Salad

Canned white beans lend flavor and texture to this nutritious, great-tasting salad. You can use any kind of cooked white bean including navy, great northern, or small white. This salad is best when chilled in the refrigerator (covered) for at least one hour before serving.

1 **large potato**
2 **carrots, peeled**
½ **pound fresh or frozen green peas**
1 **parsnip, peeled**
1 **8-ounce can cooked white beans, drained**
1 **tart apple, cored and chopped**
1 **dill pickle, chopped**
½ **cup mayonnaise**
1 **teaspoon Dijon-style mustard lettuce leaves**
1 **or 2 hard-cooked eggs, cut into 4 wedges each (make 1 crosswise and 1 lengthwise cut in each)**

1. Boil potato in skin about 20 minutes or until tender but not mushy, then chill.
2. In separate saucepans, boil carrots, peas, and parsnip until tender. If necessary, cut carrots and parsnip in half to fit in pans. Drain and chill. (Boil carrots about 15 minutes, parsnip about 10 minutes, and peas about 5 minutes or according to directions on package.)
3. Chop carrots and parsnip into bite-size pieces. Peel and chop potato.
4. In a large bowl, mix cooked vegetables, apple, pickle, and canned beans with mayonnaise and mustard.
5. To serve, arrange salad on lettuce leaves on individual salad plates. Garnish with hard-cooked egg wedges. (See page 19 for directions for cooking eggs.)

Serves 4 to 6

Tomato and Onion Tier Salad

3 medium tomatoes
2 small onions
  salt
  pepper
  dill weed

1. Wash tomatoes. Remove stems and cut into thin slices.
2. Peel onions and cut into thin slices.
3. Lay tomato slices side by side on a platter. Place one onion slice on top of each tomato slice.
4. Sprinkle lightly with salt, pepper, and dill weed and serve.

Serves 4 to 6

Rutabagas and Carrots

1 large rutabaga
6 to 8 medium carrots
3 tablespoons butter or margarine, softened
2 teaspoons all-purpose flour
1 tablespoon sugar
1 tablespoon chopped fresh parsley or 1 teaspoon dried parsley flakes
½ teaspoon salt

1. Peel rutabagas and carrots and cut into bite-size pieces.
2. In a large saucepan, bring 4 cups water and 1 teaspoon salt to a boil.
3. Add vegetables and cook about 15 to 20 minutes or until tender but not mushy.
4. Mash together butter, flour, sugar, parsley, and salt with a fork. Melt butter mixture in skillet over medium heat.
5. Drain vegetables and place in a bowl. Pour sauce over vegetables, mix well, and serve steaming hot.

Serves 4 to 6

Cauliflower, carrots, and rutabagas are three common vegetables found on Polish tables.

Cauliflower with Polish Sauce

1 medium head cauliflower

Polish Sauce:

4 tablespoons butter or margarine
4 teaspoons bread crumbs
½ teaspoon dill weed

1. Remove any green leaves from cauliflower and trim stem. Wash under cool running water. Place whole cauliflower right side up in a large kettle. Put enough water in the kettle to reach bottom florets (the ones closest to the stem) of the cauliflower and add ½ teaspoon salt to the water. Cover the kettle tightly and bring water to a boil. Cook cauliflower for about 12 to 15 minutes or until tender but not mushy.

2. In a small frying pan, melt butter over medium heat until it sizzles. (Butter burns easily so be careful not to let it turn brown.) Add bread crumbs and dill weed and stir until mixture is golden brown.

3. When cauliflower is cooked, transfer to platter. Put Polish sauce on cauliflower and serve right away by cutting off pieces with a serving spoon.

Serves 4 to 6

Orange peel and fresh marjoram put the finishing touches on chicken Polish style, a new way to prepare a familiar food. (Recipe on page 34.)

Chicken Polish Style

1 3½- to 4½-pound roasting chicken
½ teaspoon salt
1 tart apple
2 tablespoons lemon juice
4 tablespoons butter or margarine

Stuffing:

1 cup dried white bread cubes (Buy packaged bread cubes at the grocery store or make your own by cutting up stale bread.)
¼ cup milk
1 chicken liver or ¼ pound bulk pork sausage
2 teaspoons butter or margarine, softened
1 egg, separated
2 tablespoons chopped fresh dill or 1 tablespoon dried dill weed
½ teaspoon salt
¼ teaspoon pepper

1. Remove giblets from chicken and set aside liver. The remaining giblets may be used in making soup. (Giblets are usually found inside the chicken cavity wrapped in paper.) Wash chicken under cool running water and pat dry with a paper towel.
2. Sprinkle chicken, inside and out, with ½ teaspoon salt. Put on a plate and let stand in refrigerator for 1 hour.
3. Preheat oven to 500°.
4. Core and slice apple. Soak apple slices in lemon juice.
5. Soak bread cubes in milk.
6. Chop chicken liver or sausage into small pieces.
7. Cream together 2 teaspoons butter and egg yolk.
8. In another bowl, beat egg white into a stiff foam with an egg beater or electric mixer. (Egg whites beat more quickly if the bowl and beater have been chilled.)
9. To make stuffing, combine bread cubes, chicken liver or sausage, eggs, and spices. Loosely fill chicken cavity with stuffing mixture. Place apple slices on top of stuffing.
10. Grease bottom of roasting pan. Place chicken in roasting pan. Melt 3 tablespoons butter and pour over chicken.

11. Place chicken on middle oven rack and roast 10 minutes. Reduce heat to 375° and continue roasting, basting frequently, for about 1½ hours or until meat is tender. (If chicken becomes too brown during roasting, cover loosely with a tent made from aluminum foil. Make sure the shiny side of the foil is away from the chicken.) 12. Remove chicken and place on platter to serve.

Serves 4

Lemon wedges squeezed over roast stuffed fish give it a tangy flavor. (Recipe on page 36.)

Roast Stuffed Fish

Carp is a well-loved fish in Poland and is the kind most often used in this tasty dish. Whatever kind of fish you use, make sure it has been cleaned first by the butcher.

Roast stuffed fish should be prepared with the fish's head and tail left on. To serve the fish, first cut off the head and tail. Then cut the fish into thick slices, cutting right through the backbone with each slice. To remove the bones, make a slit along the backbone of each slice with a sharp knife. Lift up the side of the fish lying on top of the slit, taking it away from the bones. Then carefully pull the backbone away from the other half of the fish.

1 2- to 3-pound whole white fish
2 teaspoons butter or margarine

Stuffing:

½ pound fresh mushrooms
1 tablespoon butter or margarine, softened

2 eggs, separated
4 or 5 tablespoons bread crumbs
½ teaspoon salt
¼ teaspoon pepper

Sauce:

½ cup sour cream
½ cup half and half
¼ teaspoon salt

1. Clean and slice mushrooms.
2. In a mixing bowl, cream together egg yolks and butter with a fork.
3. In another bowl, beat the egg whites with an egg beater or fork until foamy and add to yolks. Mix in mushrooms, bread crumbs, salt, and pepper.
4. Open fish and fill the cavity with stuffing. Then fold the sides of the fish together.
5. Preheat the oven to 350°.
6. Grease the bottom of an oblong glass baking dish.
7. Melt 2 teaspoons butter in saucepan. Place fish in baking dish and pour melted butter over fish.

8. Put fish on middle oven rack and bake uncovered 40 minutes, basting frequently with drippings from fish. (If liquid in dish dries up, sprinkle fish with water.)

9. Stir half and half into sour cream, a little at a time, until smooth. Add salt and mix well.

10. Pour sauce over fish and bake 5 minutes longer.

11. Remove fish to serving plate. Spoon sauce over fish and serve immediately.

Serves 4 to 6

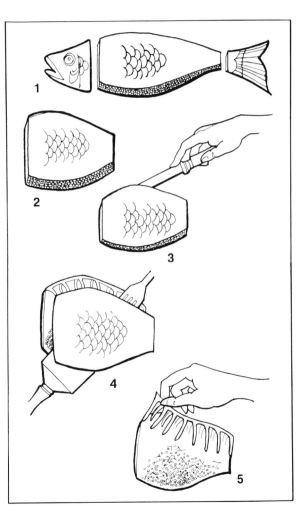

Because of the abundance of poppies in Poland, poppy seeds are used in many different foods.

Noodles with Poppy Seed

In Poland, this wonderful dish is traditionally eaten only on Christmas Eve. It is just 1 of up to 21 courses served after a day of fasting!

1 **16-ounce (1 pound) package shell or ribbon macaroni, cooked**
1 **12½-ounce can Solo® poppy seed pastry filling**
4 **tablespoons honey**
1 **cup heavy cream or half and half**
½ **cup golden raisins**
2 **tablespoons butter or margarine**

1. Cook noodles according to directions on package.
2. Meanwhile, combine poppy seed filling, honey, and cream in a mixing bowl and stir until smooth. Stir in raisins.
3. Melt butter in double boiler. Add poppy seed mixture and heat thoroughly.
4. Pour poppy seed mixture over hot, drained noodles and serve immediately.

Serves 10 to 12

Semi-Short Bread with Plums or Apricots

Dough:

2 cups all-purpose flour
½ tablespoon baking powder
½ cup powdered sugar
½ teaspoon salt
4 ounces (½ cup) sour cream
¼ cup (½ stick) butter or margarine,
**   softened**
1 egg, lightly beaten
1 egg yolk

Topping:

1 pound fresh purple plums or apricots
¼ cup powdered sugar
½ cup sour cream
1 teaspoon vanilla or almond extract
¼ to ½ cup powdered sugar for
**   sprinkling**

1. Preheat oven to 375°.
2. Grease and flour a 9- by 13-inch baking pan.
3. Wash plums, cut in half lengthwise, and remove stems and pits.
4. In a mixing bowl, make topping by blending together powdered sugar, sour cream, and vanilla.
5. In another bowl, mix together flour, baking powder, powdered sugar, and salt.
6. Cut butter into small pieces and add to flour mixture. Mash with a fork until well blended. Mixture should resemble large bread crumbs.
7. Add egg, egg yolk, and sour cream to flour mixture and mix well with your hands until smooth.
8. Spread dough evenly on bottom of pan.
9. Place plum halves skin side down on dough and press into dough. (Make sure there is some dough showing around each plum.) Put 1 teaspoon topping on each plum half.
10. Put on middle oven rack and bake 30 minutes or until golden brown.
11. Put powdered sugar in flour sifter and sift over plums. Cut into squares to serve.

Makes 18 to 24 squares

SUPPER

Supper is a much lighter meal than dinner and is eaten at about 8:00 P.M. It usually consists of bread and cheese, a light main course that can be either hot or cold, marinated vegetables, and dessert. Children and adults alike drink either hot tea with lemon or oat cocoa as they relax at the end of the day.

Vegetable Garni

Fresh green and yellow beans will add flavor and a slight crunch to this dish. If fresh beans are not available, however, you can use 8 ounces each of frozen beans instead. Cook the beans according to package directions and drain well before using.

1 pound new potatoes
½ pound fresh green beans
½ pound fresh yellow beans
½ pound baby carrots
½ medium head cauliflower

2 slices white bread
Polish sauce (recipe on p. 32)

1. Wash all fresh vegetables. If you are using fresh beans, trim off ends and leave beans whole. Peel carrots and leave them whole. Wash cauliflower and cut into florets. Boil each vegetable in a separate saucepan until crisp-tender. (Boil beans about 5 minutes, carrots and cauliflower about 10 to 15 minutes each, and potatoes about 20 minutes.)
2. Make double portion of Polish sauce.
3. Toast bread and cut into 2-inch strips.
4. Drain vegetables. Arrange each kind separately on a platter, dividing each with a strip of toast.
5. Put Polish sauce on vegetables and serve immediately.

Serves 6

A variety of carefully arranged vegetables make vegetable garni a dish that looks as good as it tastes.

"Little Pigeons" in Tomato Sauce

½ pound ground beef
¼ pound ground pork
1 egg, lightly beaten
1 medium onion, chopped
¾ cup cooked white or brown rice or
   pearl barley
½ teaspoon oregano
½ teaspoon dried parsley flakes
½ teaspoon basil
½ teaspoon salt
¼ teaspoon pepper
1 small head cabbage

Sauce:

1 6-ounce can tomato paste
1 tablespoon all-purpose flour
1½ teaspoons sugar
½ teaspoon pepper
½ teaspoon oregano
½ teaspoon dried parsley flakes
½ teaspoon basil
  pinch of cayenne pepper (optional)
1 clove garlic, minced

1 12-ounce can tomato or cocktail
   vegetable juice
1½ teaspoons olive or vegetable oil
6 strips bacon, uncooked

1. Cook rice or barley according to directions on package.
2. In a large mixing bowl, combine ground beef, pork, egg, half of the chopped onion, cooked rice or barley, and pepper and mix well.
3. Core and wash the cabbage and place in a large kettle of boiling, salted water for 10 minutes or until outer leaves become tender. Remove cabbage from water with tongs and pull off the tender leaves without tearing them. When you reach a layer of crisp leaves, return cabbage to boiling water until leaves become tender. Repeat this process until you have pulled off 10 to 15 whole cabbage leaves.
4. In a mixing bowl, combine tomato paste, flour, sugar, remaining onion, spices, and garlic. Mix well. Add tomato juice, a little at a time, and stir until

smooth. Continue stirring and add the oil.

5. Cut larger cabbage leaves lengthwise on either side of heavy center vein and discard vein. You should end up with about 20 cabbage wrappings.

6. Place 1 tablespoon meat filling at end of each cabbage leaf. Roll up leaf and bend to form a crescent-shaped roll.

7. Preheat oven to 375°.

8. Put ½ cup sauce into a deep casserole dish.

9. Place the cabbage rolls side by side in the dish, making sure they fit together tightly. Make two layers of cabbage rolls, pouring a little more sauce between layers. (Do not fill casserole dish more than halfway up the sides.) Pour remaining sauce over "little pigeons."

10. Lay strips of uncooked bacon over top layer of cabbage rolls. Cover casserole dish tightly.

11. Place dish on the middle oven rack and bake for 30 minutes.

12. Uncover dish and bake 20 to 25 minutes more or until bacon is crispy.

13. Serve "little pigeons" right from the casserole dish, spooning plenty of sauce and pieces of bacon over each helping.

Makes 20 cabbage rolls

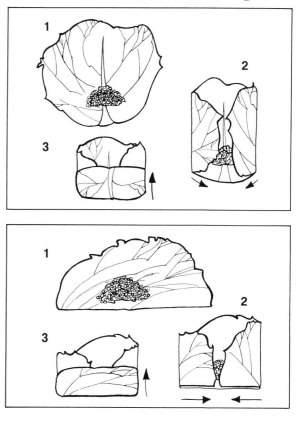

"Little pigeons" in tomato sauce, also known as gołabki (goh-WOMP-kee), are popular fare in most Polish homes. (Recipe on page 42.)

Royal *Mazurek* with Chocolate Glaze

1 cup very finely ground almonds
1 cup all-purpose flour
½ tablespoon baking powder
½ cup powdered sugar
½ teaspoon salt
4 ounces (½ cup) sour cream
½ cup (1 stick) butter or margarine, softened
1 egg, lightly beaten
1 egg yolk
chocolate glaze

1. Preheat oven to 325°.
2. Grease and flour a 9- by 13-inch baking pan.
3. In a mixing bowl, combine ground almonds, flour, baking powder, sugar, and salt. In another bowl, cream together sour cream, butter, egg, and egg yolk. Add dry ingredients to sour-cream mixture, a little at a time, mixing well each time. The dough will be stiff, so you may want to mix it with your hands.
4. Press dough into pan and place on middle oven rack. Bake 30 minutes or until golden brown. Cool in pan.
5. When *mazurek* is cool, spread chocolate glaze over top and decorate with pieces of dried fruit, nuts, citron, candied orange peel, or candy.

Chocolate Glaze:

6 tablespoons cocoa powder
3 cups powdered sugar
¼ cup whipping cream or half and half
¼ cup butter or margarine, melted

1. In a mixing bowl, combine cocoa powder and sugar.
2. Slowly add whipping cream and butter, stirring constantly until smooth.
3. Spread quickly over *mazurek*.

Makes about 24 squares

Royal *mazurek (left)* and carrot gingerbread *(right)* are two mouthwatering desserts that also make great snacks.

Carrot Gingerbread

**1 package pudding-in-the-mix
     spice cake**
¼ teaspoon ground cloves
¼ teaspoon ground cinnamon
¼ teaspoon ground nutmeg
¼ teaspoon ground ginger
¼ teaspoon ground allspice
2 tablespoons honey
2 cups grated carrots (about 6 carrots)
1 cup apricot preserves
¼ cup lemon juice
     chocolate glaze (recipe on p. 45)

1. In a bowl, mix dry cake mix and spices.
2. Make cake according to package
directions, but add honey and carrots
instead of water. Bake according to
directions in a 9- by 13-inch baking pan.
Cool according to directions.
3. In a small bowl, add lemon juice to
apricot preserves and mix well.
4. When cake is cool, cut it in half.
Place one half on a serving plate bottom
side up. Spread apricot mixture on top.
5. Place second half on top of first.

Make chocolate glaze and spread on top
and sides of cake.

Makes about 18 pieces

TEA

Although tea is not a daily tradition in
Poland, it is nevertheless a delightful—and
delicious—custom. Many Poles like to take
some time in the afternoon to go to a teashop,
where people gather for refreshment and
lively conversation. Tea is served steaming
hot in tall, thin glasses with sugar and a slice
of lemon floating on top. Coffee is served
in demitasse cups and is sometimes topped
with whipped cream. The best part of this
"snack," though, is eating one of the wonderful
Polish pastries that are baked fresh daily.
It is said that a Pole can be talked into this
quick meal at any time of the day or night!

THE CAREFUL COOK

Whenever you cook, there are certain safety rules you must always keep in mind. Even experienced cooks follow these rules when they are in the kitchen.

1. Always wash your hands before handling food.

2. Thoroughly wash all raw vegetables and fruits to remove dirt, chemicals, and insecticides.

3. Use a cutting board when cutting up vegetables and fruits. Don't cut them up in your hand! And be sure to cut in a direction *away* from you and your fingers.

4. Long hair or loose clothing can easily catch fire if brought near the burners of a stove. If you have long hair, tie it back before you start cooking.

5. Turn all pot handles toward the back of the stove so that you will not catch your sleeve or jewelry on them. This is especially important when younger brothers and sisters are around. They could easily knock off a pot and get burned.

6. Always use a pot holder to steady hot pots or to take pans out of the oven. Don't use a wet cloth on a hot pan because the steam it produces could burn you.

7. Lift the lid of a steaming pot with the opening away from you so that you will not get burned.

8. If you get burned, hold the burn under cold running water. Do not put grease or butter on it. Cold water helps to take the heat out, but grease or butter will only keep it in.

9. If grease or cooking oil catches fire, throw baking soda or salt at the bottom of the flame to put it out. (Water will *not* put out a grease fire.) Call for help and try to turn all the stove burners to "off."

METRIC CONVERSION CHART

WHEN YOU KNOW		MULTIPLY BY	TO FIND	
MASS (weight)				
ounces	(oz)	28.0	grams	(g)
pounds	(lb)	0.45	kilograms	(kg)
VOLUME				
teaspoons	(tsp)	5.0	milliliters	(ml)
tablespoons	(Tbsp)	15.0	milliliters	
fluid ounces	(oz)	30.0	milliliters	
cup	(c)	0.24	liters	(l)
pint	(pt)	0.47	liters	
quart	(qt)	0.95	liters	
gallon	(gal)	3.8	liters	
TEMPERATURE				
Fahrenheit	(°F)	5/9 (after	Celsius	(°C)
temperature		subtracting 32)	temperature	

COMMON MEASURES AND THEIR EQUIVALENTS

3 teaspoons = 1 tablespoon

8 tablespoons = ½ cup

2 cups = 1 pint

2 pints = 1 quart

4 quarts = 1 gallon

16 ounces = 1 pound

INDEX

(recipes indicated by **bold face** *type)*

ABOUT THE AUTHOR

Danuta Zamojska-Hutchins was born and raised in Warsaw, Poland. Before coming to the United States, she studied English philology at Warsaw University. Later she received her M.A. degree from the University of Minnesota, where she is now completing her Ph.D. degree in Modern Languages Education and Linguistics.

While the United States is Zamojska-Hutchins' chosen home, she still has strong ties with Poland and maintains that "you cannot fully love your new country unless you love the country that nurtured you as a youngster." Danuta visits Poland frequently for family reunions, scholarly conferences, and to do research at the many universities there.

Danuta currently teaches Slavic languages and cultures (one of which is Polish) at Buena Vista College in Storm Lake, Iowa, where she lives with her husband, Jonathan, a chemistry professor at Buena Vista College, and their two children, Edward and Maria.

Cooking has always been fun and relaxing for Danuta, and she often makes Polish feasts for her family and friends. Her other interests are oil and watercolor painting, making porcelain pottery, and creating puppets for the puppet shows she writes. She also enjoys cross-country skiing, hiking, and swimming.

Apples or pears make good substitutes in semi-short bread if fresh plums or apricots are not available. (Recipe on page 39.)